# The Genuine Poems

Poems from a Growing Heart

Dr. Lakshya Kumar Jha

BookLeaf
Publishing

India | USA | UK

Made with ❤ on the BookLeaf Publishing Platform

www.bookleafpub.in

www.bookleafpub.com

# Dedication

*For those who saw the real me,*
*even when I couldn't. Your belief*
*gave these poems breath.*

# Preface

The Genuine Poems is a collection that has been growing with me for years. They have been written over many seasons of my life, starting from my school days in class 9. Each piece captures a moment, a thought, or a feeling that felt important enough to put into words.

When I came across the BookLeaf Publishing 21-Day Poetry Challenge, I saw it not just as an opportunity to write something new, but as a chance to give life to the poems I had already written — to bring them together, to honor them, and to finally share them with the world.

What you'll find in these pages is not a polished journey from point A to point B but a genuine expression of growth, confusion, love, reflection, and everything in between. These poems weren't written with an audience in mind — they were written because I needed to write them. Each poem in this book is a reflection of something real: a moment, a thought, a feeling, or a truth I couldn't ignore. I didn't aim for perfection — I aimed for genuineness. Some poems came to me like whispers; others arrived like storms. But all of them came from a place of sincerity.

This collection doesn't follow a single theme or structure, and that's intentional. Life isn't always neat or predictable, and neither is poetry. What ties these poems together is the effort to be present, to be honest, and above all, to be genuine.

Thank you for choosing to read this collection. I hope that somewhere in these words, you find echoes of your own experiences — and maybe even the courage to express your own truths.

— Lakshya

# Acknowledgements

This collection would not exist without the quiet encouragement and support I've received over the years.

To my teachers and mentors — especially those who encouraged my writing during school — your words planted the seeds that eventually grew into this book. I still carry your encouragement with me.

To my friends — thank you for listening, reading, and sometimes simply existing when I needed inspiration. Your presence, whether near or far, has meant more than I can express in a few lines.

To BookLeaf Publishing — thank you for creating the 21-Day Poetry Challenge, which gave me the motivation and platform to bring these poems together and finally share them.

Some of the most heartfelt poems in this collection were shaped by love in its many forms — the sweetness of a first, the complexity of a maybe, and the depth of something real and lasting. Each experience, with its own joys and lessons, gave me a reason to write, reflect, and grow. I carry those chapters with quiet gratitude.

And finally, to the younger version of myself — the one who wrote these poems late at night, in between classes, or during quiet moments — thank you for being honest. This book is for you.

With gratitude,
Lakshya

# 1. Lost Angel

Had come an Angel
Into my cheerful life
To make it perhaps more cheerful,
Than it ever been had.

Memories play hide and seek
In an already junked up mind,
Loaded with moments of-
Humour, Concern, trust and kind(ness)

What was true, now turns imaginary
After leaving an impact, angel turns angry
For reason not known,
A transition seen from being known to unknown

Who was there infront each second,
Now has to be found everywhere,
Like an angel spends memorable moments,
And goes back in the skies....

Leaving me puzzled in my thoughts,
Trapped in a situation pathetic;
To search the Lost Angel in the skies,
Amongst so many stars twinkling.

# 2. Scar

So many years have passed;
Of that horrifying incident_
Now I look in the mirror
To the remnants of that scar.....

Each time I see it, my mind rewinds
Unveiling the story; hidden deep behind
Pain of the trauma had not bothered me
More than the pain post-surgery....

For the latter had inflicted on my soul
Oh God! How much I hated it that day whole;
Didn't want to see, yet saw hundred times
Why it had to happen to a beautiful piece like me....

How well stretched on my wonderful face,
Teasing me with an uncanny smile always;
Questions popping in my mind; every now and then
Even my mirror felt pity, on my eyes reddened.

Who all would accept me?
From whom should I hide it?
I laugh today on those childish tactics
Editing the images to regain my beauty...

The world was not so bad,
The way I had thought it would be.
Thanks to my family to help me step ahead,
Thanks to my friends, who were least bothered by it....

Today I am matured, person adult
So has matured my wonderful scar
Who taught me to learn along with it,
The stories of this beautiful world...

An opportunity it gave to assess,
Who loves my assets and,
Who never left despite my liability
Comforting me as if, scar had never been there...

# 3. Lost Angel 2: Illusion

Angel did return, may be in a better form
But she was not like before
She had developed a lot of regulations
Our relation was full of restrictions....

I had to be cautious this time,
Not wanted her to lose another time
Took a promise from her if something hurts
It's her duty to let me know on time...

What a wonderful time we spent
Sharing thoughts and life instead
But faith may be mine was bad
Angel didn't keep the promise we had

Again a period of sudden quietness
No information God knows what problem I have
But I do have a realisation, Angel had never returned
What went now was just an illusion....

# 4. Smiles

Are they just smiles,
Or they have a story to tell memorable?
Is it a momentary happiness,
Or a conclusion of a journey most difficult?

Are they just rejoicing,
Or feeling proud of their achievements?
Are they merely witnessing this moment instantaneous,
Or paving their path to future full of zenith?

Are they feeling loved,
Or are grateful for having been embraced atleast once?
Are they satisfied,
Or are determined to keep excelling not just once?

Are they just smiles,
Or tales of sleepless efforts?
Are their eyes just wet,
Or their each tear(drop) has its own history of
indescribable expeditions?

# 5. Lost Angel 3: Memories

A long while ago
I had a friend to me so close
Look at her :
And you forget all your sorrows,
Look at Him above :
Seemed as though by me she was borrowed

As such (things) are temporary
Damn! Her company didn't last, reason for no
How much I tried to rewind it
Poem falls short for those efforts, Oh!

Day in day out
Mind knows how to play, Oh no!!
Her beauty resurfacing time and again
Is it my mistake to not let it go?

Why they(moments) ever existed, anyone to blame?
May be He wants to mock,
For some long forgotten mistake;

Enough!! 'Tis difficult to sustain...

Angel angel please return
Your memories are hollowing me!!
Atleast let me witness your love:
While Life is gradually leaving me!!

# 6. Single

Sadness used to be engraved on her face
Today an unexpected smile prevailed I'm amazed
Though she was a tough woman
Life hadn't been much kind to her

When asked she reciprocated, Oh hey!!
Premature decisions have taken a toll of me
I learnt but, a lot from this life so pretty
Being single now feels so melancholy....

Contrasting to my desires to an extent great,
It was difficult to understand her unwitnessed pain
"I'm sorry I don't mean to intervéne
How did your choice go in vain?"

"There's no moment which has no lesson in it engraved,
Not everything can be as you, for it, pray
I'm privileged to have learnt from my mistakes
Which many in this world refuse to & disdain..."

# 7. Friendship

Mirror mirror on the wall
Tell me the ship I need to earn
To be able to conquer all the sorrows in this world
To witness the most serene affection I've ever heard

Truthful mirror on the wall
Tell me the ship I need to yearn (for)
To get the greatest sermon on bond
To reach the twin islands called selflessness and love

Oh mighty mirror on the wall
Tell me the ship I need to discern
Which would never shatter a bit in evil storms,
Of hatred, violence, pain and pun...

"Oh dear sailor of this treacherous sea:
The ship you are yearning for to earn & discern
Is nowhere to be found but everywhere rampant
Friendship is what you require
To stand up to the world high sheer high"

# 8. A Note for a Random Judgemental

My hands become such cold
That I witness death
I travel in the afterlife every other day
Which makes me cold as the snowball
Vide which children Play

I am not what you see me
I've many stories hidden within
What you read is just my stupid grin!
Ever cared to peep in my mind?
Neither did I expect to be precise...

Every day is a challenge for me
To reach its end is a feat I achieve
God did a favour I've some people with me
Who don't judge my silence as cowardice...

Oh random person, don't pass comments on me
Just because you've known me for mere minutes

I'm an open library, you've just read one sentence of it
My life though doesn't care what ye speak of me,
It just goes on whether ye care or not for me...

# 9. Unconfessed Emotions

Beyond your emojis, beyond your words,
Lies a heart, it's every beat
A pair of eyes, their innocence so clean
A stretch over those beautiful lips...

They tell another story
They talk of love, they talk of affection
Contrary to your projection,
They talk of entrusted emotions...

The insecurites ye hidden within,
The barriers ye are trapped within,
I know it's difficult but ye can try,
Just let your inner self take a sigh...

Me not forcing ye, I respect your each decision
Me not weakening ye, I trust your each gesture
Our love seldom needs a confession
One day they would resurrect from the ashes: the
unconfessed emotions...

# 10. My Valentine's Day

For me, the day you pass a smile to me
The day your eyes tell million little stories to me
The day I blush when someone takes your name
That day, becomes my Valentine's Day

For me, the day you call me to talk
The day you giggle on the other end over my flirtatious
thoughts
The day I curse the clock for being so fast
That day, becomes my Valentine's Day

For me, the day we meet away from the world
The day we talk with a hope that time would stop
The day I crack a joke and you laugh so much
That day, becomes my Valentine's Day

For me, the day you hold my hand with so much love
The day our legs caress each other under the tabletop
The day I pass my fingers through your beautiful hair
That day, becomes my Valentine's Day

For me, the day I write a new poem for you
The day I read it out, with utmost pleasure, to you
The day you say I'm your favourite poet
That day, becomes my Valentine's Day

For me, the day we hug each other
The day to my inner self emotions you impart
The day you immerse yourself into me, my heart
That day, becomes my Valentine's Day

For me, the day we kiss each other
The day our lips know no boundaries whatsoever
The day we don't see, smell, hear but just feel each other
That day, becomes my Valentine's Day

For me, the day we make love with each other
The day we charge every part of each other
The day I elevate you to the greatest height of ecstasy
That day, becomes my Valentine's Day

For me, the day you come in my dreams
The day my screen flashes with your ping
The day we both hope for a future together
That day, becomes my Valentine's Day

# 11. Self Love

They say loving oneself is selfish
They, who don't care about our good wishes...
When I am proud of what Nature has given me,
Who are they to decide what's lacking in me?

They pass comments, objectify me; thinking they are
shattering me
Never knowing(that), deep inside I'm strong, ignoring
filth...
When I and my soul know the beauty of my world,
Who are they to define what's ugly in me?

I sit infront of the only truthful piece of sheen,
An involuntary smile makes my face gleam...
I caress my scar about which they had many stories,
When I enjoy its presence, who are they to downgrade
me?

I uncloth myself layer by layer,
My eyes closed, my mind wandering into absolute

nowhere...

Feeling of my chest becoming bare, slipping of my pants
down there...

When I have so much freedom, who are they to chain me
into isolation?


My fingertips, my palms sliding into an adventure,

Sending ripples of pleasure to remotest corners of my
river...

The centrifugal build up of controlled happiness,

When I know to scale mountains though little gradual,
who are they to pull me into loneliness?


I slide my instruments along the path to heavenly
terrain,

I reach the abode of ultimate joy, so pleasant...

My skilled hands manipulating manouvres in various
proportions,

When I know my skills so much, who are they to put me
in confusion?


I escalate along the floors of ecstasy,

Regulating its intensity, sometimes upscaling sometimes
downscaling...

Setting up a rhythm and relaxing, multiple, uncountable
times...

When I know to assemble myself, who are they to tear

me apart?

I set up a final touch to my masterart...
An intense upsurge of sensations rising along my spine...
My mind lost into the infinite...
Coming back to the Planet as I find my release,
When I am so satisfied with whatever am I, who are they
to simply pressurize me and tease?

With my mind replaying the act I enacted few moments
back,
My eyes closing itself to witness a restful night...
My body falling into the lap of peace for a long while...
When I am at equilibrium with myself,
who are they to shift it without my consent?

# 12. A Ride on the Bike

The ignition turned on,
A smile waiting to find its own womb
With every race heart gains some pace,
Closer and closer to the destination...

A waiting period, a fruitful one...
A call, and I take a turn
Happiness waiting in an avatar, the best one
A pause, a companion and the ride restarts...

Today's ride is very unique
It's fuelled with touch, and sensations beneath
Half attention out of the road
Excitement rising all along 'my road'...

An image partial in the rear,
Flowers blooming spreading fragrance everywhere...
Strands of freedom rising high above
Intermingled with the image in the rear...

Those brakes in between on purpose
A shift, a clash with my inner self
Everything unconfessed yet so much expressed
Never wanting it to end, but it does extend...

Every journey has to reach an end,
Parked, ignition turned off-
Happiness and me become half-way one
Remnants persisting all around, making me smile, people
figuring out a reason!

And that the ride is now a memory
Expectations definitely engraved for the upcoming...
Each part of me thinking-
If the happiness belongs to the place twinkling...

# 13. You & Me

With every new glance of yours,
My heart skips a beat...

With every new stance on me of yours,
My soul melts in heat...

With every new breath of yours exhaled into me,
My inner self heightens to an upper being...

With every new touch of you on me,
My each cell rejuvenates in peace...

With every new bite of you on me,
My bag of pains empties itself totally...

With every kiss you implant over me,
All that is 'me', transcends into ecstasy...

# 14. Successful

You became successful the day you took your last breath,
For there are many who die each day yet have to live...

You became successful the day you went on World tour
leaving everything behind,
For there are many who have never seen the World
beyond their four walls...

You became successful the day you played with the
blood of your blood,
For there are many who get dumped in alleged 'homes'
meant for old people...

You became successful the day you took retirement,
For there are many who can't even think of doing such
stunt...

You became successful the day you got your first
promotion,
For there are many who spend their lives staying at just

one station...

You became successful the day you created your own
new self,
For there are many who wish to be creators but destiny
had other plans...

You became successful the day you married the love of
your life,
For there are many who raise children with strangers
never knowing what is love...

You became successful the day you started your first job,
For there are many who rot as educated unemployed...

You became successful the day you earned your
graduation,
For there are many who don't even get to see shadow of
college life...

You became successful the day you  confessed your love,
For there are many one sided lovers, who don't gather
courage to say what they want...

You became successful the day you went out with your
dear pals,
For there are many who don't know there exist people so

called...

You became successful the day your parents took you to the fair,
For in the same fair there are many, begging to eat some spare...

You became successful the day you entered school for the first time,
For there are many who have to work daily to build another school nearby...

You became successful the day you held that pencil and wrote your first word,
For there are many whose hands have corroded washing utensils somewhere nearby...

You became successful the day you took your first step,
For there are many who have legs but never know that they can take a step...

You became successful the day you completed 6 months of being breastfed,
For there are many who took birth but had no one to take their care...

You became successful the day you took birth,

For there are many who departed before witnessing the external world...

You became successful the day you resulted from a fruitful union,
For before your parent sperm, millions had already given up...

You become successful each 'now' you spend with excitement, satisfaction, completion & love,
For there are many living 'now' in future, dreaming to earn success by fame & chest of coins...

# 15. After Visarjan

It has ended--
The days of my celebration...
Deep within the sea
Are dissolved my memories...

To say, it was eco-friendly
But Friendship is a myth even on this eve...
While I assimilate my dissipated selves,
I see what my World has come to be...

My material self was meant to spread bliss
It can be seen today littered everywhere...
The mother(water body) I was supposed to purify,
I have corrupted her very well...

There's seldom any peace in my departure
Can't expect it from huge sound systems &
loudspeakers...
The atmosphere which shields the Mother Earth,
Fumes from crackers have breached it well...

Before I leave, I take a final glance;
All I see is garbage & it's dependants looking for some
hope around...
Confused why 'they' were created after all,
I take my leave in disappointment, what 'they' call as
Visarjan...

# 16. Dear Sister/Brother

As the patient enters the ward
You are the first to take a call
Before we even reach to them
You allot bed & make them calm

As the patient rests on the bed
You are the first to hear them out
Before we even hear to them
You pacify their soul & draw their blood (suffering)

Whenever the patient has any subtle complaint
You are the first to resolve them out
Though you let us know so we can give our advice,
The solution is always there in your mind

Whenever in the ward does anything go wrong
You are the first to get it rectified
We barely realise how does the ward run
Everything remains intact & clean, thanks to you all

There the patient cries in pain
There the taps start leaking like rains
There the ECG machine takes a break
There we can't find what is where!
You all are always there
For us in every ways...

And so we function well
Thanks to your support all the while
From documents, to mends, to every little of our
problems-
Not a moment it takes to get us a helping hand...

And then as the patient is handed over a discharge
Their gratitude though gets directed to us
But the exchange of smiles between you & them
Memories of those feeds, bed-making & tender care...
So glad that through this poetry
We thank you for always being there...

# 17. I Know You

I know you
That you are person of your words
That you think about others-
Their sorrows, grief and fears

I know you
That you are person of talent
Efficient in any work bestowed upon ya
Whether minor or anything major...

I know you
That you are person of strength
Encased within a tough barrier
But melted deep inside...

I know you
That you are person of warmth
Holding an embrace of utmost security
A company of righteous pleasure and fun...

I know you
That you are a person so so hot
Moments with you safe in memories
I know you in the most naked form...

# 18. The Intern

They come fresh in the morning
With a bundle in their hand
Of values of intricate importance
The management of those ailing on which depends

They tie the cuff round their arm
That 'whoosh' and the oscillation of the mercury
That touch and the feel of the pulse beat
Vital information served onto our sheets...

They prick their fingertips
To know the parameter to adjust the Insulins
They inject their radial
To know how long they need to be on venti...

They hold the ground avidly
By assimilating the work on a list
So as to make sure the branches branch
Of our magnificent tree...

They take that box along to the bank which mints blood
Issuing varieties of component products
Drained, sleepless and devoid of any supper
They Transfuse life into those close to their last breath...

They assist in healing a range of wounds
With time they learn number of skills
Getting hands on procedures and wits
They pool out the best out of where they exist

They become our hands and our feet
Some get close to our very heartbeat
Moments of smiles, joy and outings
They become our memories, fondly cherished
memories...

# 19. Nightingales of Surgery

At a mere blink of information
She sets up the instruments
Making sure the hall is neat and ready
She smiles when the night is merciless

Washing the ailing's agony
She dries up their pain and sufferings
Donning the linen of support
She gets all set to guide the chariot

With each hoist of the drapes
With each raise of the blade
With each clink of the instruments
She anticipates and always wins the race

There a bleeder floods the field
There the surgeon loses patience
When the junior retracts wrong
She stands out there for the rescue of all

And then things clear out for once at the end
Hands graze through the hair of still not conscious friend
Those who come out crying unstable
Not a single of them leave without smiling

And then they go on for the next adventurous journey
Taking care of the strangers name who'd be never
remembering
Once out they'll be long lost thanking many different
people
Never knowing how much they did: the Nightingale's of
Surgery

# 20. The Stranger

Not that I know you
Hardly I've known to adore you
But this conversation seems amazing
It's already making my heart a bit racing

Not that I kept any expectations
But you seem to be them already exceeding
Are you real or I'm just imagining
Pinch me before I get lost into this fantasy

Maybe I'm the echo of the wish you never said aloud,
The page you never turned — but always knew was
waiting.
If this is fantasy, then let's not return.
Because sometimes... imaginations are just truths dressed
in poetry

You spoke, and something shifted in the air —
not loud, not sharp, just... real.
Like a breeze that doesn't ask to be felt,

but still leaves the skin reminiscing.
You smiled, and suddenly time forgot itself,
pausing between heartbeats,
Like even the universe wanted to eavesdrop
on something quietly unfolding.

And now here we are —
no promises made, no futures rushed,
Just two souls slowly discovering
As if they were written together in the same ink.

I don't know where this path leads
But I know I'm not afraid,
Because with every word we have shared,
The road ahead have been feeling more like home than
unknown

You're not just a presence, you're a rhythm.
The kind my thoughts move to, even when everything
else is senseless
And maybe that's what love really is: not lightning, not
fireworks.
But a quiet voice in your soul saying to stay and to never
fade away.

That I thought my words would hardly matter
But lo, we stitched a poem together

Like the two edges healed in unison
I have become you, you've become me and there lies no
difference whatsoever.

Two edges, once distant not sewn but understood
together...
You became the verse I didn't know I was searching for
and now that you're here:
Every pause, every silence, feels like your breath resting
between my own...
We're not separate souls anymore, just echoes wearing
different names, finally meeting in a poem we didn't
know we'd already begun.

# 21. Where the Wind Nearly Held Us

We walked by the river,
Where the wind tried to steal your hair
And the sun painted everything sepia—
Like memory had slipped into the present...

The water shimmered like it knew our story,
Each ripple a page we hadn't yet turned...
You smiled at old photos,
Moments stitched in pixels and breath,
And I saw myself in your laughter,
The way it curved towards me-
Like it always meant to land there...

I teased you with a touch—
Just enough to say I'm still here,
Just enough for you to say-
That's just you being you....
And in that reply in that light,
You held more of me than hands ever could...

We didn't hold hands—
but something held us...
The wind, Or time Or the quiet miracle of knowing
someone so well,
You don't need to explain anything that I've known
everything so so well...